Arizona Myths, Fallacies, and Misconceptions

The Truth Behind Hundreds of Common Misbeliefs
about the Grand Canyon State

by John D. Neuner

**First Leaf
Publishing**

Cave Creek, Arizona

Arizona Myths, Fallacies, and Misconceptions :
The Truth Behind Hundreds of Common Misbeliefs about the Grand Canyon State
by John D. Neuner

Published by
First Leaf Publishing
28248 North Tatum Boulevard B-1 #607
Cave Creek, Arizona 85331

WWW.FIRSTLEAF.COM

10   9   8   7   6   5   4   3   2

Printed in the United States of America

LCCN: 00-191016

ISBN: 0-9669945-2-3

To my wife and daughter, for their encouragement and inspiration.

Contents

Preface

● ●

I moved to Arizona in the early 1970s. Having grown up "back east," the West, with its deserts and mountains, was very different from the sprawling suburbs and rolling farm country of my youth. I had many questions and there was much for me to learn.

Like most newcomers I was quickly educated by various "experts." (An expert is typically someone that has lived here at least a week more than you have.) I was told that palm trees are not native to Arizona. I was assured that if I was ever lost in the desert, I could cut open a barrel cactus and drink the sweet water inside. As we drove past the town of Bowie, Arizona, a fellow passenger explained that it was named after Jim Bowie, the inventor of the infamous bowie knife. On a trip to Hoover Dam, a long-time Arizona resident told me the gory tale of the construction workers that were entombed within the dam's walls.

As the years passed, I discovered that these and many other things that I was told about Arizona were wrong—myths, fallacies, and misconceptions. I soon realized that there was enough misinformation about the state to "fill a book." So I decided to write this one.

How do fallacies get started? Sometimes they are created intentionally by someone trying to color the truth. Others are based on hearsay, myths, and "old-wives tales" passed down from generation to generation. Still others originate out of faulty scientific research that has since been disproved. Once false information has been disseminated, it spreads quickly, becoming part of our collective knowledge.

How do you know if something is false? Be suspicious of statements that begin with: "Everyone knows that . . ." or "They say that . . . ." Why? Because "everyone" and "they" are frequently wrong. If something sounds strange or contrary to common sense, check it out. Find books on the subject or talk to experts. (Real experts, not the kind I described earlier.)

I wrote this book to both educate and to entertain. I limited the fallacies and misconceptions to those that can easily be disproved. I purposely avoided issues that are controversial or subject to personal opinion, religious conviction, or belief in paranormal activities. This book won't try to disprove local hauntings or debunk UFO abduction stories.

Finally, there were countless sources that I used to create this book. I would like to thank the individuals that took the time to answer what, at times, may have seemed like some very strange questions. I also acknowledge the authors of numerous books and articles that provided me with source information. I have listed many of the sources in the bibliography.

Flora and Fauna

Animals

Many people incorrectly think that Arizona is a desolate waste-land, not a place to go to see wildlife. In fact, Arizona ranks sixth in the nation in biodiversity. The state is home to 64 species of fish, 22 species of amphibians, 94 species of reptiles, 434 species of birds, and 137 species of mammals. Cougars, bear, deer, elk, coyotes, bobcats, javelinas, big horn sheep, and a myriad of other creatures roam the state's deserts and mountainous regions.

Contrary to popular belief, a snake does not have to be coiled before it can strike. A snake can strike from almost any position. Don't make the mistake of assuming that an uncoiled snake is safe.

Many people believe that baby rattlesnakes are safe to handle or are less poisonous. In fact, a small rattler's venom is just as strong as an adult's and, because they are less experienced, they may be more likely to strike. Give a baby rattler as much respect as you would a six foot long adult.

It has long been assumed that rattlesnakes, like most reptiles, do not care for their young. Recently, researchers have determined that some species of rattlers will remain with their young for the first week or two of life.

What would you do if you were bitten by a venomous snake? Years ago people were told that they should cut open the wound and suck the poison out. Some sources also recommended that a tourniquet be applied above the wound to prevent the venom from spreading. Camping supply stores even sold "snake bite kits" that contained a small sharp knife, a suction device, and a tourniquet.

This "cut and suck" method is no longer recommended. Today most experts recommend that you should keep the victim calm and take them to a hospital emergency room as soon as possible. The victim should avoid walking or unnecessary movement because this increases blood flow and enables the venom to spread more quickly.

In the old western movies a cowboy would be walking down a trail, minding his own business. Suddenly a rattler would leap from a nearby rock. Wham! The unsuspecting cowpoke is struck in the leg. Is this how snake bites really happen? Actually, no. The majority of rattlesnake bites are the result of someone molesting or attempting to capture a snake.

A false belief about rattlesnakes is that every bite is venomous. The truth is that no venom is injected in about one quarter of all bites.

There are many myths about ways to tell a poisonous snake from a nonpoisonous one. Contrary to what many believe, triangle-shaped heads, heavy bodies, cat-like pupils (vertical slit), or rough scales can be found on both venomous and nonvenomous snakes.

You may have been told that you can identify a poisonous coral snake if you remember the poem: "Red on yellow, kill a fellow, red on black, venom lack." Don't bet your life on it! It's a common misbelief that you can positively identify a coral snake by looking for a red band next to a yellow band. If there's a red band next to a black band, the snake is supposed to be nonpoisonous. The truth is that there are harmless snakes with red bands next to yellow bands and some coral snakes have very little red coloring on their upper surfaces. If you want to identify any of Arizona's numerous species of snakes, buy a good field guide.

If someone tells you that the coral snake's venom is the most toxic of any Arizona animal, please correct them. Drop for drop, the harvester ant's venom is more toxic than any of the state's other creatures. It's even more toxic than a king cobra. Fortunately, harvester ants inject such a small amount of venom that they are not considered dangerous. (A word of caution about all bites and stings: In rare cases, a person could have an allergic reaction to an insect bite or sting that could fatal. If someone develops a rash, has difficulty breathing, or has any other unusual symptoms after any bite or sting, seek immediate medical attention.)

Some people think that rattlesnakes shake their rattles for several reasons: they rattle to call potential mates; a rattle signals other snakes to come to their aid; the rattle's sound and motion is used to confuse or "hypnotize" prey. All of these beliefs are false. The only purposes of the rattle is to warn other animals to stay away and to distract predators.

Everyone knows that snakes can't bite while they're in water—right? Wrong! If it feels threatened, a snake will bite, even if it's swimming. However, because it can't get a foothold on anything, it is unable to strike very far.

How do you repel rattlesnakes? Carry white ash? Carry an onion? Burn some old shoes? Surround your campsite with jars or other glass objects? Rub your boots or clothing with oil from a king snake? Although all of these have been recommended at one time or another, none have any basis in fact.

The number of beads on the rattle does not indicate a snake's age in years. Rattlesnakes form a new bead each time they molt (shed their skin), but this can occur more than once a year. It's also possible for beads to break off. However, there is one thing that you can tell if you are able to count the number of beads —you're too close to the snake!

ψ

There are many other popular myths about rattlesnakes. Here are just a few: A rattler must remove its poison glands to drink. Alcohol counteracts the venom and a drunk person is immune to snake bites. Rattlers never bite children. A rattlesnake will never strike a person from the rear. Rattlesnakes must lick their prey to moisten it before they can swallow it. In addition to small animals, rattlers also eat berries or cactus fruit. Rattlesnakes are fond of milk. All of these statements are false.

ψ

In Arizona's warmer regions, Indian house crickets seem to be everywhere during the summer months. People that have moved to the state in the last 20 years or so probably assume that they've always been here. In fact, these ubiquitous creatures are not native to the state. The first specimen to be described in the literature was found in Ceylon (now known as Sri Lanka) many years ago. The first time they appeared in the United States was in 1877 when several of them were identified in the southeast. In 1948 one was found in Arizona. Some sources say that an isolated colony of these creatures lived in the utility tunnels of the University of Arizona for years. Then, in the late 1970s, they suddenly left the tunnels and quickly spread throughout the state. This story has since been debunked and no one is really sure how they got here. But, since they've arrived, they've spread quickly in the last few decades and now can be found in and around most Arizona homes.

Cicadas are responsible for that buzzing sound you hear in the desert during the warmer months. If you moved to Arizona from the eastern United States you probably thought that cicadas lived underground for 17-years before emerging. For the species of cicada found in the northeastern United States, that's true. As with many other things, life in the desert is a little different. Arizona's lower elevations are home to a another species, the Apache cicada, that has a much shorter three-year life cycle. Cicadas are sometimes incorrectly called "locusts." Locusts are a type of specialized grasshopper, unrelated to cicadas.

Tell some people that you've found several scorpions in or around your house and they may tell you that you "have a nest of them somewhere." To get rid of them you have to locate and destroy the nest. Contrary to what many people believe, scorpions do not form nests. It is true that groups of bark scorpions can be found hiding together in one location, such as under a piece of tree bark, but they are not nesting.

ψ

Scorpions do not have pinchers on the ends of their arms. In fact, they don't have any real arms at all. Those appendages that look like arms are highly modified mouth parts.

ψ

Did you find a drowned scorpion in the bottom of your swimming pool? Don't be too sure. Although the scorpion may appear lifeless, it may suddenly become active once it is taken out of the water and allowed to dry out. Some scorpions can be submersed in water for up to two days without drowning.

ψ

Don't assume that a small scorpion can't inflict a deadly sting. In fact, one of the smallest species found in Arizona, the bark scorpion, is the most dangerous. Thousands of Arizonans are stung by scorpions each year. While fatal scorpion stings are very rare, in years past, scorpions killed more people in Arizona than all rattlesnake bites combined. Fatality rates are much lower now thanks to the development of antivenom. (In Mexico where emergency medical care is less available, it's estimated that as many as 500 to 1,000 people die each year from scorpion stings.) Small children, the elderly, and people with health problems are most likely to have a serious or life-threatening reaction to a sting.

ψ

A misconception about scorpions is that newly born baby scorpions attack, kill, and devour their mothers. The truth is that the mother scorpion carries her newborns on her back for a week or two, until their first molting. After they molt they climb down and head off to live on their own, leaving the mother unharmed.

Growing up to two inches in length, the American cockroach —commonly called a "sewer roach"— is an all-too-common visitor to Arizona households in the warmer months. Many people mistakenly believe that they enter a home through the sewer pipes. Although they can live in the sewer system, they rarely enter a building by climbing up drain pipes. All drain pipes contain a u-shaped trap that holds water and keeps odors and bugs in the sewer from entering a building. It is very unlikely that a roach would, or could, swim through a water-filled trap. If you find a roach in your home it probably came from outside, entering your home by crawling under a door or through a crack. (Roaches can crawl through an opening as thin as a dime.) Since they are drawn to water, roaches are often found near sinks, toilet bowls, shower stalls, and bathtubs. When you see a roach crawling out of your drain, it probably crawled into it from your house, not from the sewer.

Some people will tell you that a tarantula is capable of leaping several feet. Although they move very quickly for short distances and seem to pounce on their prey, tarantulas don't jump.

ψ

Mention the word tarantula and everyone envisions a huge spider. You may be surprised to learn that not all tarantulas are large. Thirty species of tarantulas live in Arizona. While some species grow as big as a man's fist, others grow no larger that a half dollar.

ψ

In the movies, you may see a particularly sinister villain try to kill someone by releasing a tarantula near them—usually into the victim's the bed while they're sleeping. Waking up to find a tarantula crawling on you would not be a pleasant experience, but you'll survive. While their bite is painful, it is not life threatening. Using fangs that can be as large as a cat's incisors, tarantulas do inject a venom into their prey. Although this venom can kill or incapacitate an insect or other small animal, the bite is not considered dangerous to humans. Another myth about tarantulas is that they only eat insects.

Until recently even "tarantula experts" believed this. It's now known that they also feed on small snakes, lizards, and small rodents.

The solpugid is a large, spider-like creature found in Arizona's desert regions. It is also known as a sun spider or wind scorpion. An old wive's tale claims that if a solpugid drowns in an animal's water bowel or trough, it poisons the water. Any animal that drinks the water will die. Not true.

Some sources report that the only two dangerous spiders in Arizona are the black widow spider and the brown recluse spider. In fact, true brown recluse spiders do not live Arizona. However, Arizona is home to two similar species of spiders, which are commonly referred to as brown spiders. The bite of these brown spiders can be just as hazardous as that of the brown recluse.

Arizona is home to a venomous lizard known as the gila monster. If provoked, it can inflict a painful and potentially life-threatening bite. There are many myths about these unique creatures. Among them are: If they bite you they won't let go until sunset. If they bite you they won't let go until they hear thunder. They have no rectum and they are poisonous because of the buildup of waste material in their bodies. Their breath is toxic. If you get too close they will spit poison into your eyes.

Africanized ("killer") bees have been found in Arizona for several years now. Despite their nickname, "killer" bees do not hunt for things to attack. When they do attack, it's because they sense that something is a threat to their hive. You may have heard that Africanized bees can sting more than once or fly faster than other bees. These are just myths. They are like other bees, but considerably much more aggressive.

If you are attacked by bees, do not try to protect yourself by staying in one area and swatting at them. Dead bees produce an odor that excites other bees and this may cause even more of them to attack. Submerging yourself underwater is not a good idea either; the bees will be waiting for you when you resurface. You should get away from the hive and seek the nearest shelter, such as a house or car. If there is no shelter available, just keep running away from the hive. The bees will eventually stop chasing you. If you have been stung multiple times seek immediate medical attention.

Arizona is home to a wide variety of animal life. Despite what you may think or have been told, many of these critters are newcomers to the state. The following is a partial list of Arizona animals that many people believe to be native species when, in fact, they are not.

Mammals

House mouse

Norway rat and black rat

European ferret

Bison (American buffalo)

Wild horse and burro

Opossum

Fish

White sturgeon

Freshwater eels

Coho and sockeye salmon

Rainbow, cutthroat, golden, brown, and brook trout

Northern pike

Carp

Bigmouth, black, and smallmouth buffalo fish

Channel, flathead, blue, black, yellow, and brown catfish

Mosquito fish

Striped, white, yellow, smallmouth, spotted, and large mouth bass

Bluegill

Green and redear sunfish

Crappie

Walleye

Yellow and Sacramento perch

Ciclid

Reptiles and Amphibians

Bullfrog

Softshell turtle

Clawed frog

Marine toad

Mediterranean gecko

Birds

Starling

House sparrow

Rock dove (domestic pigeon)

Chucker

Invertebrates

Crayfish (crawdad)

These non-native species came to the state under a variety of circumstances. Some species, such as gamefish, were introduced for the benefit of sportsmen. Other species were introduced inadvertently by someone that brought a specimen into the state and released it. In many cases, no one knows exactly where or when a new species was first introduced. Some of these non-native animals are benign and have little impact on the ecosystem. In other cases the introduction of a new species has threatened the survival of native species.

Javelinas are not wild pigs. The javelina is a collared peccary, which is not even in the same zoological family as a pig.

Another common misconception about javelinas is that they are dangerous and will charge and attack people. The truth is that javelinas are fairly timid creatures. Although they will attack if threatened or harassed, they prefer to avoid confrontations.

Arizona has been home to two types of bears — the grizzly bear and the black bear. In the early part of the twentieth century, grizzly bears were purposely hunted to extinction in the state. Black bears can still be found throughout much of Arizona. Despite the popular belief, bears do not hibernate (reducing their metabolism, heart rate, and respiration) as some animals do. Some bears become inactive during the winter and "den-up," but they do not go into a state of hibernation. Other bears remain active throughout the winter months.

Did you think that all black bears have black fur? Although most black bears are black in color, some have a brown or tan coat.

Cougars (mountain lions) are frequently killed to protect livestock. Although cougars will attack livestock, their impact has been greatly exaggerated. Domestic dogs actually kill many more livestock than cougars. Are they a threat to humans? If you believe the old western movies, you would think that people were constantly being attacked by cougars. In truth, cougars prefer to avoid human contact. Between 1890 and 1990 there were only 20 recorded cougar attacks on humans in the United States. With rare exceptions, cougars will not bother humans unless they are molested or feel threat-ened.

If you encounter a cougar you may think that running away is your best bet. Experts believe that it's best to remain calm and hold your ground. If the cat does not retreat, and you think that you should, do so slowly and confidently. Running is what the cougar's natural prey would do and this may trigger an attack by the cat. If a cougar does become aggressive you should make yourself seem as large and as threatening as possible. Shout, bang a metal pot, wave your arms over your head, or swing a tree branch back and forth. Don't follow the advice that's often given for bear encounters and become passive by curling-up or laying on the ground. By lowering yourself to the ground you may seem more vulnerable. Remaining in a upright position seems to discourage these cats. A jogger that was recently killed by a cougar wasn't attacked until he bent over to tie his shoe.

Did you think that Arizona was a place where "the deer and the antelope play?" You can see deer play in Arizona but not antelope (unless you're at the zoo). Arizona is home to pronghorn sheep that are commonly—but incorrectly—called antelope or pronghorn antelope. In actuality, there are no true antelope in North America. True antelope species are only found in portions of Asia and Africa.

Although elk are commonplace in Arizona's higher elevations you won't find any elk that are native to the state. While it's true that elk, in the generic sense, are native to the state, the elk that are here now are not. Native elk were of a type known as *C. e. merrimi*. This elk is extinct in Arizona—killed off by hunters by the 1920s. The elk that are currently found in the state are of a different type *(C. e. nelsoni)* and were transplanted, by man, from other parts of the country.

Did you know that coyotes aren't carnivores? Although their normal diet consists mainly of meat, as much as 40 percent of their diet can consists of plant material. Technically, coyotes are omnivores (plant and meat eaters).

Another mistaken belief about coyotes is that they mate for life. They don't. Both parents do participate in raising their pups, however.

People that have captured a desert tortoise to keep as a pet know how interesting these docile creatures are. What they may not know is that they are breaking the law. Many of the animals found in Arizona, including tortoises, are protected by Arizona law. If you capture or molest them, you could end up paying a hefty fine or even being sent to prison.

If you find a tortoise in the desert, don't assume that you have not harmed it if you handle it, then release it. Tortoises store water in their bladder, allowing them to survive dry periods. When threatened, they often empty their bladder, attempting to startle a predator with this sudden squirt of water. If you pick one up it may try this trick on you. Unfortunately, once the bladder is emptied, the tortoise has lost this vital water reserve and may die from dehydration. Remember, the desert is not a petting zoo. If you see one of these creatures, observe it from a distance.

What some people call "horned toads" or "horny toads" are really reptiles, not toads. Because of their short, flat bodies and small legs, they look like toads. The correct names for these peculiar creatures are the horned lizard or desert spiny lizard. Several species of these unique reptiles are found throughout the Arizona deserts and can even be found in mountainous terrain at more than 5,000 feet of elevation.

Has someone told you that horned lizards can squirt a stream of blood from their eyes? As strange as it sounds, it's true. When threatened, they do this in an attempt to confuse or startle a predator. They also have another strange defense. Some species of horned lizards can puff themselves up with air to make it more difficult for a predator to eat them.

If you watched Roadrunner and Coyote cartoons as a child you know that the coyote would use birdseed (usually ACME brand) to lure the roadrunner. In the real world this would never work. Most people are surprised to learn that the roadrunner is a swift and cunning predator that feeds on lizards, snakes, insects, and other birds. Another little known fact about roadrunners: Although they spend most of their time on the ground, roadrunners are capable of flying for short distances.

If you have a hummingbird feeder you may have been warned not to leave it up all year. Why? It's commonly believed that the birds will become dependent on the feeder and forget to migrate. Don't worry, there are hummingbirds that live in Arizona year round and you can leave your feeder up all of the time. When it comes time for a bird to migrate, it will, whether your feeder is there or not.

Another fallacy is that the feeder solution must be red in color. It's true that hummingbirds are attracted to the color red, but as long as the feeder is red in color, the solution does not have to be.

When people find baby animals alone in the desert or forest many incorrectly assume that they've been abandoned. Many species of animals found in Arizona leave their young alone while they hunt for food. Deer, for example, may leave their young alone for hours at a time. If you do find a young animal and you are certain that it has no parents, or if it is injured, contact a wildlife rehabilitator or the Arizona Game and Fish Department. These sources can either take care of the animal or advise you on what you should do.

When you were a kid did your parents tell you not to touch a baby animal because its mother would smell your scent on it and reject it? Sorry—mom and dad were wrong. Although you should avoid handling any young wild animal, it's okay to return a fallen baby bird to its nest.

Have you seen any black widow spiders around your house? Anyone that has lived in Arizona for any length of time would probably answer "yes." Well, technically speaking, you haven't. Scientists defined a black widow spider as the species *Latrodectus mactans*, which is normally found only in the east. Similar species of spiders, which are common to Arizona, are called "widow spiders." But, unless you're a scientist, it's OK to call the ones you find in Arizona, "black widows."

Whether you call them black widows or widow spiders you probably thought that they are called "widows" because the female spider always kills the male spider when the two mate. This is a commonly held misbelief. The truth is that the male black widow often escapes from the affair unharmed. If the male is killed, it is not as a result of the mating process. During mating the female temporarily suppresses its predatory instincts. Once mating is over, these instincts quickly return. The male, which is much smaller than the female, soon begins to look more like food and less like a mate. The unfortunate male that remains near the female after mating will probably be killed and eaten, just like any other small creature that crosses the female spider's path.

Centipede means "100 feet" so you may have thought that they have 100 legs. The name is misleading. Centipedes can have as few as 28 legs or more than 300 legs. Centipedes in Arizona can grow nine inches long. They have large, powerful jaws that can inflict a painful bite. While they are venomous, their bite is not considered to be dangerous to humans. Centipedes are typically seen at night in the state's desert regions. Although their diet consists mostly of insects, this species of centipede's menu is not limited to other bugs. At times, they will dine on small lizard, toads, and even rodents.

Like the centipede, the millepede's name is inaccurate. Millipede means "1,000 feet." However, even a large millepede will only have a few hundred legs.

Despite what you may have been told, the feet of the centipede are not poisonous. Their legs have sharp tips on them and they can puncture your skin if they crawl over you. In some cases these tiny puncture sites may become inflamed or infected. This has led some to mistakenly assume that the centipede's legs have injected them with some kind of venom.

If a woodpecker is banging on a metal object it's not because it's stupid and can't figure out that it is not made of wood.

The woodpecker is trying to make as much noise as possible. Woodpeckers bang on objects to attract mates or warn other woodpeckers to stay away from their territory. They'll seek out objects that make the loudest noise and, much to the annoyance of its occupants, will often bang on a house's chimney or metal cooler.

You may have heard that the Sonoran desert toad is poisonous and then assumed that you want to avoid being bitten by one. These toads (sometimes called Colorado River toads) are commonly found in Arizona's deserts during the summer monsoon season. While their bite is not poisonous, the toads secrete a potent toxin from their skin. Touching a toad will not make you sick but you should wash your hands thoroughly afterward. Don't touch your mouth or eyes until you have washed your hands. Never allow small children to handle these toads. They might put their hand into their mouth after touching it and ingest some of the toxin. If a dog licks or mouths a toad they can become temporarily paralyzed or even die. Wash its mouth out thoroughly with running water and contact your veterinarian. If you find a toad in your dog's water bowl, rinse the bowl and replace the water. If you find one in your yard, and you have young children or outdoor pets, it's best to remove it.

Did you think that a minnow is a small fish? The Colorado River is home to a very unusual member of the minnow family, the Colorado squawfish. While most minnow species are less than five inches in length, the squawfish can grow as large as six feet and weigh more than 70 pounds. At one time this giant could be found in many western rivers from Wyoming to the Gulf of California. When the water from these rivers was diverted for agriculture and other uses, much of the squawfish's natural habitat was eradicated. Today this fish is on the endangered species list and can only be found in a few locations.

Plants

The tumbleweed—a classic icon of the American West. You probably thought that these unique plants careened across the western landscape for centuries. If so, you'll be surprised to learn that the correct name of the tumbleweed is the Russian thistle and that it originates in the Russian steppes. A newcomer to the states, it was probably brought to this country by settlers from that region. It is thought that the Russian thistle seeds were mixed in with flax seed that immigrants brought to America to cultivate.

Have you heard about Arizona's famous jumping cholla cactus? Some believe that its branches are capable of jumping onto a passerby. Don't worry, cactus plants won't bother you unless you touch them or bump into them. The jumping cholla's arms are covered in very fine, very sharp needles. You only have to brush against it lightly to get stuck. Because the needles are covered with small barbs they adhere to your skin or clothing. If you pull away suddenly (which you probably will) a piece of a branch may break off and stick to you. When this sticking-pulling-breaking chain of events occurs, it almost seems like part of the cactus jumped onto you.

ψ

Palm trees are a common site in Arizona's warmer urban areas. Almost all of these trees have been imported into the state or grown in local nurseries. A commonly held belief is that there are no palm trees that are native to the state. In fact, you can find native fan palms growing wild in the southwestern portion of the state and in a small region northwest of Phoenix. These palm trees were here long before the first landscaper set up shop.

Some people think that the century plant is so named because it lives 100 years, blooms, then dies. In fact, this normally slow-growing plant can live from 10 to 75 years. When it blooms it can grow as much as a foot a day, sending out a stalk that will reach a height of 15 to 30 feet. Contrary to the popular notion, century plants don't necessarily die after blooming. The leaves may die but the roots can live and grow a new plant.

Don't refer to yuccas, ocotillos, or Joshua trees as cacti (or cactuses). These desert-dwelling plants are not cacti but are members of the lily family.

When the desert is bulldozed to make way for urban growth, developers often remove some of the saguaro cacti and transplant them to other areas or sell them. Since they are not destroyed in the bulldozer's wake, you might assume that these saguaros have been saved from destruction. Unfortunately, mature saguaros frequently die when transplanted. For very large saguaros, the mortality rate can be as high as 90 percent. This death does not usually happen right away but may take up to five years to occur.

Despite the fact that a saguaro cactus can grow more than 30 feet tall, it is not, as some believe, the tallest cactus in the world. The cardon cactus, found in Sonora, Mexico frequently exceeds 50-feet in height.

Bermuda grass, commonly found in Arizona lawns, is not from Bermuda. It actually came from Africa and India.

Many people mistakenly believe that cacti should be planted in the winter when there's less stress from the heat. In fact, winter is the least favorable time to transplant a cactus. Winter rains cause the soil to be damp and this can lead to root infections. Also, because many cacti are dormant during colder weather, they are less able to fight an infection. If you have a choice, transplant during the warmer months.

If you plant native Arizona plants in your yard, don't presume that natural rainfall will provide them with enough water. If they are planted in an area that mimics natural desert conditions that may be true. However, most homeowners plant native plants more densely than would occur in the wild. This makes them compete with each other for water. In such cases, supplemental watering may be necessary.

Cactus spines are not poisonous. They can cause an infection˝ or inflame the puncture site, but they are not coated with a toxic substance.

Did you think that the desert is the only place that you will find a cactus? Although they are not as common as they are in the desert regions, cacti can be found throughout the United States. Vermont, Maine, and New Hampshire are the only three states, in the 48 contiguous states, where you cannot find native species of cactus.

Is the saguaro cactus endangered? Are they slowly dying due to diseases, air pollution, or holes in the ozone layer? For several decades alarming rumors like this have been circulating. The truth is that Arizona's saguaro populations are fairly healthy and there is no indication that they won't continue to thrive.

ψ

It's widely believed that a saguaro cactus grows its arms so that it will balance itself. The truth is that the arms grow at random and some of these giants will have all of their arms on the same side.

ψ

Xeriscaping is the term used to describe landscaping with plants that require very little water. Desert residents are encouraged to use xeriscaping instead of traditional landscaping such as a lawn. Does xeriscaping always save water? In many cases the answer is no. A recent study discovered that homeowners with xeriscaped property often used more water than homeowners that had irrigated lawns and shrubbery. The problem is that many Arizona residents are new to the idea of xeriscaping and over-water their low water usage plants. People need to realize that when it comes to desert plants, a little water can go a long way. If done properly, a xeriscaped area will use much less water than a traditional grass lawn.

ψ

Cotton is not new to Arizona. It's believed that early people grew cotton here over 2,000 years ago.

ψ

While most people think of a barrel cactus as a short, squatty plant (hence the name), some can grow to over 10 feet tall.

ψ

Living in the Desert

• •

Ask someone to describe a desert and they will probably say that it is a hot, dry region. That description is half right. Deserts are defined by aridity or "dryness," not by temperature. In some deserts freezing temperatures are common. It may be surprising to learn that Antarctica contains regions that meet some scientists' definition of a desert.

Tucson is not located in the desert? What? That's heresy!! Tucson prides itself on being located in one of the most beautiful parts of the Sonoran Desert. However, there is currently much debate among biologists about whether the Tucson area is really a desert. The climate and ecosystem found in this area does not meet the strict definition of a desert. A more accurate classification of this region is "thornscrub." Many believe that the area will be officially reclassified from desert to thornscrub in the near future.

You've probably heard a recent transplant to Arizona make a statement like: "I love Arizona, but I miss the seasons." While Arizona's desert regions don't experience frigid winters and hot humid summers, the southwestern deserts do have their own seasons. The Tohono O'odham tribe believed that there were twelve seasons and gave them names like "Small Rains Moon" and "Big Cold Moon." The Arizona-Sonora Desert Museum (located near Tucson) recognizes five seasons:

Spring (February - April): Wildflowers, wind, and sporadic rainfall.

Foresummer or Dry Summer (May - June): Hot and dry.

Summer Monsoon (July - Mid-September): Hot with thunderstorms.

Fall (Mid-September - November): Dry and warm.

Winter (December - January): Mild with gentle rains.

ψ

A mirage occurs when light rays are bent by variations in air density and temperature. Mirages are frequently seen while driving on flat stretches of open road. As you look into the distance you see what appears to be a puddle of water on the pavement. As you approach, the water disappears or recedes into the distance. Travelers in the desert can experience similar phenomena. Tempting pools of water seem to lie a short distance ahead. As they get closer, the water vanishes. Despite the popular notion, mirages are not limited to deserts or other hot locales. They can occur in cold climates as well.

Another misconception about a mirage is that it is a hallucination. Hallucinations occur when your brain fools you into thinking that you see or hear something that does not exist at all. A mirage is an optical illusion, not a hallucination. Your eyes actually see the mirage. A mirage can be photographed, a hallucination cannot.

ψ

At times, the air in many parts of Arizona has unhealthy levels of particulates (dust particles). Some assume that this condition can't be avoided because we live in a desert. But not all arid regions have high levels of dust and particulates. Natural desert soil produces very little dust compared to soil that has been disturbed by construction or agriculture. Dust control measures, such as pre-wetting construction sites and paving dirt roads, can significantly reduce the amount of dust released into the air.

ψ

So, you're out four-wheeling in the desert and your truck breaks down. What do you do? Head downhill because that's where you might find water? Walk back down the road and try to find your way back? Climb a nearby peak so that you can get a better view of the surrounding terrain? In most cases all of those actions are the wrong things to do. Although every circumstance is different, most experts recommend that you remain with your vehicle. There are several reasons why it is best to stay put rather than wander off. Your vehicle can provide you with shelter. Your horn, headlights, or mirrors can be used to signal for help. You can burn a tire to make a very visible signal fire. Finally, it's much easier for search-and-rescue teams to spot a vehicle than a person walking in the desert. In many cases, rescuers will find a lost person's vehicle long before they find the lost person. In far too many instances, the person is found dead from exposure and probably would have survived had they stayed with their vehicle. One more reason to stay: You'll need more water and overheat faster if you're walking than you will at rest. (An impor-

tant side note: Whenever you hike, bicycle, or drive in a remote area, always tell someone where you are going and when
you intend to return. They should be instructed to call the
local authorities if you do not return at the designated time.)

How much water do you need to hike in the desert? A quart
should be plenty—right? Studies have shown that a healthy,
conditioned person can only travel about 10 miles on flat
terrain in 110 degree heat even if they drink a quart of water
along the way. After ten miles, dehydration and exhaustion
will set in, making it difficult to continue. If the same person
carried an entire gallon of water they could probably travel
about 15 miles before they got into trouble. Ten or fifteen
miles may seem like a long way, but if you become lost or
disoriented, you can quickly cover that much ground trying
to find your way back. (note: These amounts were determined using healthy subjects under controlled conditions.
The water requirements for any given individual can be quit
different.)

While hiking in the desert you may think that you should fight your feeling of thirst and try to make your water last as long as possible. Not a good idea! Although you never want to waste water, most desert survival guides tell you not to stringently ration or hoard your water. People have died from dehydration, yet still had water in their canteens. If you have water—drink it.

On the other hand, is it possible to drink too much water? Surprisingly, yes. If a person drinks a lot of water and does not eat anything, they can dilute the electrolytes in their blood. This can lead to a condition called water intoxication (hyponatremia). Water intoxication is serious and potentially life threatening. Always bring something to snack on when you go for a hike. Drinking a sports drink such as Gatorade® can also reduce the risk of water intoxication.

After you've been in a warm climate for a few weeks your body adapts to the higher temperatures and you can tolerate the heat better. People commonly think that's because the warmer climate "thinned their blood." Not true. Blood doesn't thin in warm climates or thicken in cold ones. This is an "old wive's tale."

You've probably heard that you can cut open a cactus and drink the water inside. Don't count on it! The water inside a cactus is contained in a gooey, pulpy substance that includes bitter and potentially toxic alkaloids. If you do manage to swallow some of it, there is a good chance that it will make you vomit or have diarrhea—neither of which you want to do if you're already dehydrated. There is one species of barrel cactus that contains a small amount of a drinkable fluid, but you'll have to squeeze it out of the pulp. It's a lot of work, and you may lose more fluid from sweating than you'll be able to extract from the cactus. Don't count on a cactus to be your emergency water reserve; always bring enough water for your desert excursions.

You don't have to be lost in the desert to die from the heat. Every summer there are reports of children or animals that become ill or die because they are left in parked cars. These tragedies occur because somebody had the mistaken belief that if they crack the windows, and only leave for a few minutes, that the child or pet would be okay. People underestimate how quickly the interior of a car can heat up. Even with the windows partially open, the interior of a car can reach 100 degrees in just 10 minutes on an 85-degree day. That's a mild day for many parts of Arizona. If it's 105 degrees outside, a car's interior can exceed 200 degrees in the same amount of time. Never leave your pet or child in a parked car.

You may have been warned to leave your car windows down slightly during the Arizona summer. "If you don't, the air in the car will expand and blow a window out." Car windows can shatter from the heat but it's not because the air in your car expands like a balloon and pushes them out. Even with the windows closed, a car is not airtight. There are many openings, cracks, and vents that allow air to escape. Windows burst because the glass expands and pushes tightly against the window frame. In very rare cases, the glass pushes with enough force that it shatters.

You probably thought that you sweat less in Arizona than you would in a humid climate. Actually, you may be sweating more here, but just don't notice it. In a humid climate sweat does not readily evaporate. It beads up on your skin and soaks your clothing. In an arid climate sweat quickly evaporates from skin and clothing, so they appear much drier.

ψ

If you've lived in the Arizona desert for a couple of years you may have been told that you've probably had Valley Fever already. Valley Fever or "cocci" are the common names given to *coccidiomycosis*. This disease is caused by a fungus that is native to the soil of the southwest deserts. When infected, most people experience mild flu-like symptoms. In fact, without medical testing, you can't tell the difference between most cocci infections and a cold or flu. Occasionally the symptoms can be severe and even life threatening.

Contrary to what many people believe, your chance of getting Valley Fever is only about 1 in 30 each year that you live in an area where the fungus is found. If you're an adult and have lived in Arizona most of your life, you've probably had it. If you're a newcomer, and lived here only a few years, you probably haven't. People that work in a dusty environment, such as construction or agriculture, are more likely to contract the disease. Your doctor can give you a skin test that will determine if you've ever had it.

Another common misconception is that you can only get Valley Fever once in your life. While this is true most of the time, there are documented cases of people that have had repeat infections.

People, Places, and Politics

● ●

Famous People and Places

Geronimo spent much of his life in the Arizona Territory and is often described as a cunning warrior and a great Apache chief. The fact is that Geronimo was not a chief. He was a shaman or "medicine man." Geronimo wasn't even his name. The name Geronimo (Spanish for "Jerome") was given to him by the Mexicans. His Apache name was Goyathlay which means: "one who yawns."

Did Robbie Knieval really jump across the Grand Canyon on a motorcycle? Actually, no. He jumped a side canyon which one spectator described as nothing more than a "big drainage ditch." Although the distance between the takeoff and landing points was about 220 feet, the distance between the two ramps was only about 150 feet. Nationwide television audiences were told that if he failed in his attempt, that he would have fallen over 2,000 feet to his death. In fact, the distance to the bottom was less than 200 feet. It was a spectacular, death-defying jump, but it was not over the Grand Canyon.

Drive along Arizona Highway 79 about 20 miles south of Florence and you may notice a roadside marker made of rocks and topped with the statue of a horse. This often overlooked structure is the Tom Mix Memorial and marks the location where the famous western movie star died in an auto accident in 1940. There are many rumors about the details of Mix's accident. These include: Mix was driving a Rolls Royce with longhorn cattle horns attached to his hood. (It was a Cord—no horns.) Mix was towing Tony the Wonder Horse when the accident occurred. (Nope.) Mix's car was struck by a truck carrying a load of silver dollars. (Mix was speeding and lost control of his car when he encountered a construction zone. He ran off the road.) Although Tom Mix is probably one of the most well known movie cowboys, he and his publicist frequently made up of false stories about his past to make him seem more colorful. Mix claimed to have been a former Texas Ranger and to have fought in the Boer War. Neither of these claims are true.

During World War II America used Navajo Indians to translate messages into a secret code based on the Navajo language. This prevented the Japanese from decoding these transmissions if they were intercepted. The "Navajo Code Talkers," as they came to be known, are credited with saving many lives by keeping our secret military communications from falling into the hands of the enemy. However, contrary to what most people think, this was not an original idea. During World War I, America used Choctaw Indians to relay coded messages.

As a child did you sing the nursery rhyme: "London Bridge is falling down, falling down. . . ?" Did you go to Lake Havasu to see that famous bridge? If so, that's not the bridge you saw. The London Bridge that the nursery rhyme refers to was built in the twelfth century. Over the years it was damaged by several fires and was often in a state of disrepair (that's why the rhyme says that it's "falling down"). It was eventually dismantled in the 1800s. The bridge that is currently in Arizona was one that was built to take the place of the original "London Bridge."

The O.K. Corral in Tombstone is one of Arizona's most well-known tourist attractions. Each year, countless tourists visit this site to see the place where the most famous gunfight in history took place. Unknown to most of these visitors is the fact that the gunfight did not occur at the O.K. Corral. It actually took place down the block in a vacant lot next to Fly's Photography Studio.

There are skeptics that will tell you that Boot Hill Cemetery, located near Tombstone, is not a real cemetery. They believe that the markers are fakes, designed to attract unwitting tourists. In fact, Boot Hill is a real cemetery and at least 250 people are buried there. For many years the graveyard was not maintained and many of the original wooden grave markers were stolen, destroyed, or decayed. They were eventually replaced with new markers and in some cases they may not be in the exact locations of the original ones. Although most of the epitaphs are the same as those on the original markers, a few may have been added or changed when the new markers were created.

ψ

Over 20,000 people visit Fountain Hills, Arizona, each year to see what is billed as the "World's Tallest Fountain." Under ideal conditions, when all three of the 600-horsepower pumps are activated, they shoot a geyser of water over 500 feet into the air. Although the fountain is always a spectacular sight, visitors to this unique attraction will rarely see it reach this height. Only two of the pumps are usually active and the average height of the fountain is only about 330 feet. Although many people still call the Fountain Hills Fountain the world's tallest, it lost that title several years ago. In 1995, the city of East St. Louis built the Gateway Geyser, which is 600-feet tall.

ψ

Have you been told that the westernmost battle of the Civil War was fought in 1862 at Picacho Peak, Arizona? While many insist that this statement is true, others debate its accuracy. The controversy stems from varying definitions of the word "battle." Some say that another Civil War engagement that occurred at Stanwick Station, 100 miles farther west than Picacho Peak, was the westernmost battle. Others disagree, claiming that, unlike the Battle of Picacho Peak, the Stanwick Station fight was not a "real battle," but was more of a "skirmish." However, some historians do not classify the Picacho Peak fight as a battle either. Less than 25 soldiers were involved in the Picacho Peak "battle." Despite these debates, historians agree that the "Battle of Picacho Peak" was Arizona's most significant Civil War conflict and worthy of its place in Arizona's history books.

Located in one of the hottest parts of the state with cells made from solid rock, the infamous Yuma Territorial Prison made today's prisons look like country clubs. You may hear people claim that no one ever escaped from Yuma Territorial Prison. The fact is that 26 people escaped from the prison and were never recaptured.

Old Tucson is not located on the original site of the city of Tucson. This famous western movie set and theme park wasn't even built until 1939.

ψ

It's been said that Arizona's Petrified Forest National Park contains wood that has "turned to stone." Don't believe it. Wood cannot turn to stone any more than a stone can turn to wood. Petrified wood is actually a fossil of wood. When wood is buried in an area where there is water and a high concentration of the right minerals, these minerals will seep into the wood's fibers. Over time, the minerals build up inside the wood, then harden. After many years a stony structure is formed in the shape of the wood. Sometimes this petrification process is so precise that you can actually see the fine detailed structures of the original wood fibers.

If you visit Petrified Forest National Park don't assume that it's okay to take some petrified wood as a souvenir. Although the park estimates that it loses tons of petrified wood every year, it's against the law to remove even a small piece. If the fear of a fine is not enough to deter you, consider this. A popular legend warns that petrified wood stolen from the park is cursed. Every year the park has pieces mailed back to it from people that claim that their stolen "souvenir" brought them nothing but bad luck.

Mission San Xavier del Bac, often called the "White Dove of the Desert," is a beautiful 200-year old mission located near Tucson. It is a must-see for anyone visiting the area. Mystery surrounds the mission because one of its two bell towers was never completed. If you ask local residents why the tower is missing you may hear several different stories. Some will tell you that a construction worker fell to his death while working on the tower. Because of the death, local Indians believed that the tower was cursed and refused to work on it. Others may tell you that the Spanish crown did not tax missions until they were completed. The builders purposely left the bell tower unfinished in an effort to avoid taxation. Still others contend that the tower was finished but it was struck by lightning and destroyed. Historians most familiar with mission claim that none of these reasons are true. They believe that the builders simply ran out of money. After many years of construction the project had accumulated a lot of debt. Without money to continue, construction was halted. In fact, the bell tower is not the only part of the mission that was never completed, it's just the most visible.

Hundreds, possibly thousands, of people have searched for the legendary "Lost Dutchman's Mine." Located in the Superstition Mountains east of Phoenix, the mine is supposed to contain a fortune in gold. If the mine does exist (and there's a lot of evidence to suggest that it doesn't), will it make its finder rich? Unfortunately the land on which the treasure is supposedly located belongs to the federal government and mining or mining claims are prohibited. If the treasure is found the only person who will become richer is Uncle Sam.

Place Names

Arizona's name is not the result of combining "arid" and "zone." Although the origin of "Arizona" is uncertain, most historians believe it was named after some springs located 85 miles south of Tucson, in what is now Mexico. The local Indians called these springs Aleh-zon, which means "small spring."

Bowie, Arizona, was not named after Jim Bowie (of Bowie knife fame). Bowie was named after nearby Fort Bowie, which was named after Colonel George Bowie of the Fifth California Infantry Volunteers. A little know fact: Although he made the Bowie knife famous, Jim Bowie probably did not invent

65

it. Many historians believe that it was actually designed by Rezin Bowie, his brother.

You may have assumed that Phoenix's Broadway was named after Broadway in New York, or that like so many other cities, Phoenix decided to name a major street Broadway. In fact it was named after a person, Noah Broadway.

William "Buckey" O'Neill was a noteworthy person from Arizona's past. He was mayor of Prescott, a sheriff, and even rode with Teddy Roosevelt's "Rough Riders." For some reason there are those that think that the town of Buckeye was his namesake (despite the fact that the names are spelled differently). The town was named Buckeye because many of the early residents came from Ohio, the "buckeye state."

You may have thought that the town of Cornville is a place where corn is grown. According to some of the earlier settlers, the residents intended to name the town Cohnville after the Cohns, a family that lived there. (Some sources spell the name Coane or Cone.) Officials in Washington misspelled the name on the town's official documents, calling the town Cornville. Rather than going through the trouble of having the name corrected, the town residents decided keep the name Cornville.

Ed Cave, also known as "Rackensack," was a well-known and colorful character that lived around the Cave Creek area of Maricopa County in the late 1800s. It's often assumed that the town of Cave Creek was named after him. According to the Cave Creek Chamber of Commerce, the town was named after a small creek that flows near a wide, open-mouthed cavern.

The Grand Canyon's name does not refer to the grandiose nature of this vast chasm. Many years ago the Colorado River, which flows through the canyon, was named the Grand River. The canyon was named after the river.

Almost a mile wide and 600 feet deep, Arizona's Meteor Crater is an impressive site. The name Meteor Crater is scientifically incorrect though. The word "meteor" describes an aerial phenomenon only. It is the light that occurs when one of these "space rocks" burns up in the atmosphere. When it falls to earth it is called a meteorite. Because the crater was formed by a massive object that slammed into the earth, it should have been named Meteorite Crater. Meteors don't strike the earth, meteorites do.

ψ

The San Francisco Peaks on the outskirts of Flagstaff contain Arizona's highest point, Humphrey's Peak. It has been said that the peaks got their name because some believed that you could see the city of San Francisco from the summit. In fact, the peaks were named in honor of Saint Francis by Spanish missionaries in the 1600s.

Montezuma's Castle is a 5-story, 20-room cliff dwelling located near Camp Verde, Arizona. Early settlers believed that the structure was built for the Aztec emperor Montezuma. It was actually built by the Sinagua Indians and was abandoned about 100 years before Montezuma was born.

When you hear the name Happy Jack you probably think that this Arizona community was named after some jovial character that lived in the area. It was actually named after a place in Wyoming.

When driving between Phoenix and Tucson on Interstate 10 you pass McCartney Road. For years a rumor has circulated that the road was named after Paul McCartney. Although the former Beatle does own property in the Tucson area, McCartney Road was named in the 1930s after a local family.

Pinetop is located high in the pine and fir forests of Arizona. It's only natural to assume that the town was named to describe its location. Pinetop was actually named after Walt Rigney, a local saloon keeper. Rigney had a very noticeable fuzzy lock of red hair and his nickname was "Old Pinetop." When Fort Apache soldiers wanted to visit saloon they would say, "Let's go see 'Old Pinetop.'"

It snows in Snowflake during the winter but that's not why the town's early residents decided to give it that name. Snowflake was named after two men who lived there. One was Erastus Snow, the other was William Flake.

ψ

Tuba City wasn't named after the musical instrument. It was named after a Hopi chief.

ψ

Geology and Geography

Neither Tucson's "A" Mountain nor Picacho Peak are extinct volcanic cinder cones. Many people think that they are because of their shapes.

ψ

Travelers between Phoenix and Tucson must pass over a sandy depression in the desert called the Gila River. Those not fa-

miliar with the state's history may wonder why something
that is dry most of the time is called a river. Before Roosevelt
Dam was built, diverting its water, the Gila used to flow from
New Mexico across Arizona all the way to the Colorado River.

ψ

If you think that Arizona does not have earthquakes you are
mistaken. Earthquakes in Arizona are rare, and generally mild,
but they do occur. Many quakes felt in the state originate in
Mexico or California. In fact, the state is rated as a having a
moderate earthquake risk because of its proximity to those
regions. The earliest documentation of an earthquake in Arizona is of those occurring at Fort Yuma in the mid-1800s.
One of the most noteworthy earthquakes occurred in 1887
and was centered about 200 miles south of Tucson, near
Bavispe, Mexico. This trembler caused damage to buildings
in several Arizona cities and could be felt as far north as Al-
buquerque, New Mexico. Another strong earthquake occurred
in January 1907, the same year as the great San Francisco Earthquake. Flagstaff experienced some strong shocks during this
quake. A series of 52 earthquakes occurred in September 1910.
A 1912 quake created a 50-mile-long crack near the San Francisco range and damaged buildings in Williams. Several strong
tremors occurred in 1935 shaking the residents of Welton
(near Yuma) and damaging houses in northern Arizona. In
1950, another quake left large cracks in the ground in Apache

County. Since 1950 several small quakes have been felt but none that have caused significant damage.

ψ

Some claim that the Grand Canyon is not the deepest gorge in the country. They say that Hell's Canyon in Idaho, which is 7,900-feet deep, is about one-half mile deeper. The problem is that you can't really compare the two. The Grand Canyon is a massive gorge cut into relatively flat terrain. Hell's Canyon is located in a mountainous area and its apparent tremendous depth is due to the presence of the surrounding peaks.

ψ

There are many legends and myths about the Grand Canyon. One legend, that started many years ago, is starting to be retold in recent years. The legend arose out of a 1909 article in the Phoenix Gazette. According to the article, Professor G.E. Kincaid, an archeologist from the Smithsonian Institute, discovered a huge underground citadel buried deep within the walls of the Grand Canyon. Within this vast, man-made cavern he found mummies, sophisticated metal tools, and elaborately carved statues. There was a large stone idol that looked like statues of Buddha found in the far east. He also saw hieroglyphic writing on the wall that was similar to the hieroglyphics used by the ancient Egyptians. The place was so large that he estimated that 50,000 people could have lived comfortably within it. In some cases this citadel extended for more than a mile underground. This is an incredible story but there's one problem with it—the Smithsonian Institute has no record of this find and there was never a Professor Kincaid on their staff during this time period.

This story has taken on a more modern twist in recent years. Rumors are now circulating that the United States government has built an elaborate system of tunnels within the Grand Canyon's walls. These tunnels do not contain mummies and artifacts, but are being used to store nuclear missiles and other military paraphernalia.

"When California slides into the ocean, we'll have beachfront property in Yuma." This remark is a running joke among Arizonans. Western California is part of the Pacific Continental Plate, and through a process known as plate tectonics, is moving at the rate two inches a year. Most people think that it's sliding westward into the sea or that a major earthquake will cause it to fall into the ocean. Unfortunately for surfers in Yuma, California is sliding to the north, not westward.

The next time your out-of-town visitors complain that there's too much desert in Arizona, ask them if they'd like to see the tundra. "Tundra in Arizona? . . . surely you're kidding!" Tundra, typically associated with places like Alaska and northern Canada, is only found in regions that have very cold winters. Because it's so cold, the only vegetation that you'll find in a tundra are small bushes or other low-growing plants. Trees are unable to survive. High atop Arizona's San Francisco Peaks is a small region of alpine tundra where you can find some of the same types of plants that live in Alaska's arctic tundra. However, don't expect to find any polar bears there—just cold air and a fantastic view.

Many people are surprised by the number of lakes that an arid state like Arizona has. Well, they're not natural lakes.

Stoneman Lake in northern Arizona is considered by many to be the state's only permanent natural lake.

Politics

Although Arizona is predominantly a Republican state, you may be surprised to learn that it was not always this way. Most Arizonans were Democrats up until the last few decades. As one Democrat complained, "We didn't have any Republicans in this state until they invented the air conditioner." Even today, the Tucson area is predominantly Democratic.

Ask most Arizonans what the colors are on the state flag and they will say they are red, yellow, and blue or that it's red, yellow, blue, and gold. In fact, the star in the middle is supposed to be copper, symbolizing Arizona's once powerful copper industry. It's hard to dye cloth to look like copper so many people aren't aware that it's supposed to be a copper star.

ψ

Despite what your friends may have to told you, it is not illegal to drive barefooted in Arizona. This is a common misconception.

ψ

If you're one of the Arizonans that doesn't register to vote because you don't want to get picked for jury duty, your plan won't work. In Arizona, potential jurors are selected from both voter registration and drivers' licenses databases.

ψ

If you hear someone say that Prescott used to be the state capitol, please correct them. People that make this statement have the right idea, but they are technically incorrect. What they should have said was that Prescott used to be the capitol of the Arizona Territory. In 1889, the territorial capitol was moved from Prescott to Phoenix. Arizona did not become a state until 1912. The state capitol has always been Phoenix.

Arizona was the 48th state to join the union. However, it was not (as many people incorrectly proclaim) the last of the states in the continental United States to join. Alaska, which became a state later, is also on this continent. The term "continental United States" is often used incorrectly to mean all of the states except Alaska and Hawaii. The correct way to describe those 48 states is to refer to them as the contiguous states of the United States or the lower 48 states.

Dumb or Strange Laws

From time to time talk shows, magazines, and newspapers will run a piece entitled "strange laws" or "dumb laws." These are unusual or outdated laws that supposed to be "still on the books." Listed below are Arizona dumb or strange laws that were gathered from various sources. Each law was reported to be still in effect. As you will see, none of the sources bothered to check the facts.

Dumb Law: In Arizona there is a law that specifically makes it illegal to hunt camels.

There is no such law in the state statutes. The Arizona Game and Fish Department, which regulates hunting in the state, has no regulations pertaining to camels.

Dumb Law: Any misdemeanor committed in Arizona while wearing a red mask is considered to be a felony.

There is no such law in the Arizona Statutes.

Dumb Law: In Tucson, it is illegal for women to wear pants.

There is no such law on the books in Tucson. Around the turn of the century, a law made it a misdemeanor offense for someone to appear in public in the dress "not of his or her sex." Although pants were not specifically mentioned, it is possible that some may have interpreted the law to mean that women cannot wear pants.

Dumb Law: In Globe, it is illegal to play cards in the street with a Native American.

Although there may have been a law like this in the territorial days, there is currently no such law, and the city clerk's office in Globe did not recall there ever being a law like this.

Dumb Law: In Glendale, it is illegal to drive a car in reverse.

Both the Glendale City Attorney's Office and the Glendale Police Department report that there is no such law in effect.

Dumb Law: In Nogales, it is illegal to wear suspenders.

The Nogales City Attorney's office reports that there is no such law in effect and they could not find any documentation that there was ever was a law like this.

Arizona Residents, Economy, and Lifestyles

Have you been told that Arizona has more boats per capita than any other state? This claim has been circulating for years. In fact, Arizona is not even in the top ten in terms of boat ownership.

Many people assume that Arizona's urban areas are responsible for using up the limited amount of water that's available in the state. Arizona's homes and businesses actually use only a small portion of the state's water supply. Most of the water (about 80 percent) is used by agriculture.

Because Arizona is a great place to retire and is home to many large retirement communities, many believe that Arizona must have one of highest concentrations of senior citizens. In fact, when states are ranked by their percentage of elderly residents, Arizona is not even in the top ten. Surprisingly, the state is currently ranked seventh for its percentage of teenagers.

Beautiful weather year-round, hundreds of golf courses, hiking trails, and parks—Arizona residents must spend much of their time outdoors, enjoying all that the state has to offer. The truth is that a recent study determined that Arizona ranks last in the nation when it comes to physical activity.   Who would have thought that this state has more "couch potatoes" that any other in the nation?

People with allergies and respiratory diseases often come to Arizona expecting that the dry, clear air will help them. After moving here, many find that their symptoms have actually worsened. Arizona's urban areas are notorious for their high levels of airborne pollens.   In Tucson, the number of people with allergy problems is double the national average. Where is all of this pollen coming from? Natural desert vegetation is not to blame. The major culprits are olive trees, mulberry, trees, and Bermuda grass lawns.

ψ

Arizona is one of the fastest growing states in the country. Conventional wisdom says that most newcomers are from the eastern or midwestern states. The truth is that most newcomers are from the southern and western parts of the country.

ψ

Many urban Arizona residents complain about traffic congestion. "Traffic is terrible. It's getting as bad as Los Angeles!" Although the Phoenix and Tucson areas do have traffic problems, it may not be as bad as you think. Many other urban areas in the nation are much worse according to the Texas Transportation Institute. When comparing the amount of time people are stuck in traffic, Phoenix ranks 35th in the nation . On the average, a Phoenix area resident can expect to waste 35 hours a year due to motor vehicle traffic. Tucson ranks 42nd and Tucsonians spend 28 hours stuck in traffic per year.

Compare those numbers to Los Angeles where commuters can expect to spend 82 hours each year in traffic jams.

In Arizona's early days cotton, copper, cattle, and citrus were considered to be the backbone of the Arizona economy. While everyone knows that these industries have become less important, it may be surprising to learn that agriculture currently accounts for less than 2 percent of the state's exports. Mining products account for less than 1 percent.

What's the top commercial crop in Arizona? Everyone know that it's cotton, . . . right? Wrong! The average Arizonan will be surprised to learn that it's lettuce.

It's often said that the states of Arizona and Hawaii do not change to Daylight Savings Time during the summer. The truth is that parts of Arizona, located on the Navajo Reservation, do switch to Daylight Savings Time.

What is the most affluent community in Arizona? Many people still think that Scottsdale is. While Scottsdale is home to many of the state's "movers and shakers" it is not the richest community to live in. That title doesn't even go to Carefree, an even more exclusive town to the north of Scottsdale. If you really want to rub shoulders with Arizona's rich and famous, move to Paradise Valley located northeast of downtown Phoenix. However, before you start collecting cardboard moving boxes and preparing to move there, make sure you have a small fortune saved up. The median price of a home in Paradise Valley is $750,000!

Since so much of the state is desert, one would assume that drownings occur infrequently in Arizona. On the contrary, drownings are a frequent occurrence in the state and Arizona has the one of the highest rates of infant and early childhood drownings in the nation. Most of these occur in backyard swimming pools.

A popular Arizona cuisine is the Navajo Taco (also known as the Indian Taco). Ask anyone in Arizona, including many Native Americans, and they will probably describe it as a traditional Navajo food. What most people don't know is that the Navajo Taco was invented in Arizona by a Greek restaurateur in the early 1960s.

Did you think that the chimichanga came from Old Mexico? While its exact origins are often debated, there is general agreement that the first chimichanga was created in Tucson in the 1950s.

Weather

Heat

The movies and television sometimes portray the western deserts as places where you'll bake in 110 degree temperatures during the day, then encounter freezing temperatures at night. If you've lived here any time at all you know that's not the way it is. A 100-plus degree day is not followed by a freezing cold night. During the winter months desert temperatures can drop well below freezing at night. However, the daytime temperatures are much lower during these months as well. During the hot summer months, when daytime temperatures are high, nights are mild with low temperatures typically in the 70s and 80s.

Arizona's "dog days of summer" can be a sweltering time of the year. The origin of the term "dog days" is typically misunderstood. They are not called the "dog days" because of the way dogs become inactive and lay around in hot weather. The term "dog days" was first used by the early Greeks and Romans. During the hottest summer months the star Sirius, which the ancients called the "dog star," rose with the morning sun. These ancient astronomers thought that the "dog star" was the cause of the hot weather, so they called late summer the "dog days." Because the stars shift slightly each year, relative to the earth, we no longer see the conjunction of Sirius and the sun during the summer months. However, we continue to call late summer the "dog days."

When most people think of Yuma they imagine sweltering heat and think that it's one of the hottest cities in the state. It is routinely the brunt of heat-related jokes. "If you want to know what hell is like, you just need a sense of Yuma." It's been described as the "town that winter forgot." Legend has it that a soldier from Yuma died and went to hell. It was too cold for him so he went back to Yuma to get some blankets. In 1872 the *Arizona Sentinel* said that Yuma residents "stand in the Colorado River half the day and stay drunk the rest of the time to avoid death by melting." But hold on a minute— if you live in the Phoenix area you should be careful before you criticize Yuma. It will be surprising for most Arizonans to learn that during the last ten years, the average summer temperature in Phoenix has been higher than that of Yuma. "So . . . , did you hear the one about the soldier from Phoenix that died and went to hell . . . ."

The Sun

In many parts of Arizona residents enjoy more than 300 sunny days a year. Within those warm rays lies a hidden danger. Because of the abundant sunshine, Arizona has one of the highest rates of skin cancer in the country. A widely held belief is that sunscreen will protect you from the danger of excessive exposure to the sun. Although suncreens are an important part of your arsenal in the defense against skin cancer, they do not offer complete protection. Some skin-damaging, cancer-causing ultraviolet rays will still reach your skin. If you have to be in the sun, experts recommend that you also wear a wide brimmed hat, pants that cover your legs, and a long-sleeve shirt whenever possible.

Don't let a cloudy day give you a false sense of security. It's true that ultraviolet (UV) exposure will be reduced by 50 percent or more on a rainy or overcast day. However, on partly cloudy or thinly overcast days, the amount of UV radiation you receive can be about the same as on a cloudless day.

The state's higher elevations are known for their cool temperatures, which offer a welcome respite for those seeking to escape the sweltering desert heat. When the temperatures are cooler, it's often assumed that the sun's rays are less intense. Actually, the suns rays can be more damaging at these higher altitudes. UV-B rays (associated with skin cancer) can be 60 percent higher in the mountains compared to sea level. This is because the air is thinner and allows more UV radiation to pass through. If you live in the mountains, or plan to visit them, be sure to wear sunscreen and avoid unnecessary exposure to the sun.

Some people don't wear sunglasses, claiming that "the sun doesn't bother my eyes." Even if the sun doesn't seem to bother you, it could be causing permanent damage to your eyes. Studies have shown that exposure to UV rays is one of the risk factors associated with the development of certain types of cataracts. Another eye disorder, macular degeneration (the leading cause of vision loss in elder Americans) is also associated with UV exposure. Pterygium is a growth that occurs on the white of the eye. It is found more often in people that work outdoors and are exposed to sun and wind. If left untreated it can lead to vision loss. Enjoy Arizona's sunny climate—but wear your sunglasses .

Just because your sunglasses claim to block UV radiation, don't assume that they are protecting you adequately. The American Optimetric Association recommends sunglasses that absorb 99-100 percent of both UV-A and UV-B radiation. Unfortunately, it is not always easy to find eyewear that provides this much protection. Some manufacturers do not provide labels that indicate the level of UV protection and some labels are misleading. Be wary of labels making vague claims such as, "blocks harmful UV rays." The label should clearly indicate the percentage of UV rays that are absorbed. It may be surprising to learn that the cost of eyewear does not determine how much protection is provided. A recent study found that some expensive sunglasses did not provide adequate protection while some inexpensive brands provided complete protection.

Arizona's summers are not the hottest part of the year because the earth is closer to the sun. In fact, the earth is closer to the sun during the winter (in the northern hemisphere). Summertime is hot because the angle of the sun to the earth is more direct, causing the sun's rays to be more intense.

Storms and Rain

Many think that Arizona is nothing but a big desert and that it receives very little rain. It's true that many of the desert regions can expect less than 5 inches of rain each year. Davis Dam, Arizona, holds the record for the least amount of rainfall in the state. In 1956 it received only 0.07 inches of rain. Phoenix's driest year was 1956 when it received only 2.82 inches of rain. However, other parts of the state can expect significant rainfall. Communities located at higher elevations will receive 25 to 30 inches of precipitation each year. The record for the most precipitation occurred in 1978 when Hawley Lake received almost 59 inches of precipitation.

Since it's so dry you would think that the desert would soak up rainwater like a sponge. In fact, the opposite is true. Most desert soil is compacted and contains very little organic material. It actually absorbs water very slowly. Ninety-five percent of rainwater is lost to runoff, evaporation, or is quickly absorbed by thirsty plants. Only the remaining five percent remains in the ground to recharge the groundwater supply.

What's the best way to drive across a flooded street or wash? Do you drive slowly so that the water doesn't splash into your engine compartment? Maybe you should drive fast so you keep up your momentum. Is it best to drive in the middle of the road because it's shallower there? If you're smart you won't pick any of these options and will stay out of flooded roadways. If a low section of the street is flooded or a flooded wash is in your path—avoid it. The water may be deeper than it appears or could rise rapidly. Every year many motorists do not heed this warning and end up stranded in, or atop, their partially submerged vehicles. Sometimes the water rises before rescuers can arrive and drownings occur. Those that are rescued can look forward to a bill for the cost of the rescue. If you ignore warning signs and enter a flooded area, the state of Arizona and many local governments can require the motorist to pay the cost of the rescue—and it's not cheap.

If there are storms in the area, but they are many miles away, don't think that it is safe to be in a wash or ravine. This misconception has cost far too many lives in Arizona. Storm surges can travel many miles and flash floods can occur in areas that have received no rain at all. The flooding occurs suddenly and is often described as a "wall of water." Even if a storm is occurring miles away, stay out of ravines, streams, and washes.

Arizona's monsoon thunderstorms are known for their intense lightning displays. They are exciting to watch, but they can be deadly. Never assume that you're safe from lightning just because there is no lightning in the clouds directly over you. Lightning can travel great distances. After someone is struck by lightning, witnesses will often say that the strike was unexpected. "The storm seemed to be far away, we thought that we were safe here." If there's lightning in the area, stay indoors.

It's been said that Arizona's summer monsoon season starts on July 4th. Unfortunately mother nature is not that predictable. The monsoon season typically starts in mid-July but this can vary considerably from year to year. In Phoenix, the monsoon season has started as early as June 19th and as late as July 25th. Many consider it to have officially arrived when there are three or more consecutive days of dew points averaging at least 55 degrees.

Just because the summer monsoon season has started don't assume that heavy rains are sure to come. Although some summer monsoon seasons deliver upwards of nine inches of rain, in other years, less than an inch of rain may fall during the entire monsoon season.

If you want to use the term monsoon correctly, don't say: "We had a bad monsoon last night, it blew down one of our trees!" The word "monsoon" refers to the seasonal change in prevailing wind patterns, not to the storms themselves. A correct expression would be: "We had a bad monsoon thunderstorm last night!"

ψ

Dust storms or "haboobs" are common occurrences during Arizona's summer monsoon season. Dust storms are formed when downdrafts in a storm cell hit the ground and are deflected out toward the front of the cell. These winds pick up dust particles from the soil creating huge clouds of thick dust. The average maximum wind speed within a dust storm can exceed 30 miles per hour and dust clouds can extend up to 3000 feet into the air. If visibility is limited by a duststorm, some drivers will pull onto the shoulder of the road and turn their lights on. They believe that their lights make them more visible and will prevent someone from crashing into them. Don't make this mistake! Leaving your lights on during a dust storm, while parked on the side of the road, can actually increase your chances of being hit. When visibility is low drivers tend to follow the taillights of the vehicle in front of them. If you're on the shoulder with your lights on, drivers behind you may assume that you're still moving and attempt to "follow" you. The result: you get rear-ended.

Dust devils are frequent sights in the southwestern deserts. Typically these "mini-tornadoes" contain winds that average about 25 miles per hour. Scattering dust and debris, most people consider them to be a harmless nuisance. What you may not know is that they can be quite destructive. On rare occasions a dust devil's wind speeds can approach 100 miles per hour and can tear the roofs off of buildings.

Tornadoes may not occur in Arizona as frequently as in other parts of the country, but they do occur. On the average, three tornadoes are sighted each year in the state. There are many myths about what to do if a tornado is in the area. One recommendation was based, in part, on a book written in the 1800s. At that time it was believed that the side of the house facing the tornado received less damage. Because tornadoes frequently approach from the southwest, people were advised to go to that corner of a building. More recent research indicates that the side of the building facing an oncoming tornado may be the least safe. Experts now recommend that you shouldn't head toward a particular side of the building. Instead, you should go into a small windowless room, on the lowest floor, near the center of the building. Bathrooms are usually a safe room because they are well framed and the pipes in the walls may add some additional strength. Also, bathrooms usually don't have large windows that can shatter, spraying broken glass.

Don't assume that a car will protect you from a tornado. While a car can provide you with protection from many other weather-related threats, it offers little protection from the awesome power of a tornado. Most sources recommend that you abandon your vehicle and head for the nearest building. If no buildings are nearby, seek out the lowest place around such as a ditch or culvert. Lay flat on the ground. Never try to outrun an approaching tornado in your car.

There are those that believe that the mountainous areas of the state are safe from tornadoes. While tornadoes may be infrequent in higher elevations, no place is safe from their threat. In the 1980s, a tornado in Yellowstone National Park traveled up and down a 10,000 foot-tall mountain.

When the temperature drops in Arizona's colder regions you may hear the weatherman say things like, "It was 30 degrees today but with the windchill it dropped to 10 degrees." If you don't understand windchill you might assume that the air temperature was 10 degrees. It wasn't. Wind chill does not affect the air temperature. The windchill factor was developed to determine the effect of wind on exposed human flesh. When air is blown over human skin it draws heat from the skin and this chills the body. The stronger the wind, the faster the body chills. That's why it feels so good to sit in front of a fan on a hot summer day. However, windchill does not make the air and other inanimate objects colder. A rock in your yard is just as cold on a 40-degree day as it would be on a day when the thermometer reads 40 degrees, but the windchill factor is 5 degrees. Windchill does not change the air temperature, it just feels colder when it's windy.

Urban Legends

● ●

What is an urban legend? Unlike the "legends of old," an urban legend takes place in the modern times. Like any legend or myth, the source of an urban legend is never well defined and when it spreads, the story often takes on different forms. Most urban legends either have a humorous side or describe some ghastly event. Sometimes the tale involves a little of both. Frequently the victim in the story (if there is one) is seen as being punished by a horrific death brought on by their own arrogance or foolishness. Many other urban legends describe some secret, unethical activity undertaken by the government, a celebrity, or "big business." Although some urban legends are complete fabrications, many of them have an element of truth. Finally, an urban legend has to be a good story—after you hear it, you can't wait to tell your friends about it. After all, it's a "true story."

The Urban Legend: In 1976, two polar bear cubs escaped from Tucson's Reid Park Zoo by crawling into a nearby sewer pipe. Over a ten-year period, Tucson residents spotted the pair several times, as they poked their heads out of sewer drains.

This legend, which some have called "The Saber Bears of Tucson," is Arizona's own version of New York's "Alligators in the Sewers" urban legend. In reality, no polar bear cubs have ever escaped from the zoo.

The Urban Legend: Most of the resort hotels built in Arizona in recent years have been prewired for slot machines and other casino equipment.

This urban legend has been circulating for several years. Supposedly these hotels want to be prepared for statewide legalized gambling. By prewiring the hotel, they can turn them into casinos in a matter of weeks. A Phoenix television station recently tried to determine if this was true. None of the resorts that were contacted had done any prewiring for casino equipment.

The Urban Legend: A woman noticed that a large saguaro cactus in her yard was quivering. She had never seen anything like this before. The woman quickly called a local nursery and described what she was witnessing. The nurseryman told her, rather frantically, that she should call an exterminator, then leave the area as fast as possible. As she was pulling her car out of her driveway, the saguaro suddenly stopped quivering, made an abrupt jerking motion, then burst open. Thousands of baby scorpions spilled out. She was told later that scorpions sometimes lay their eggs inside a cactus and it will appear to move as the newly hatched babies struggle to get out.

In some versions of this story baby tarantulas pour out of the cactus. Either way, it has no factual basis. Neither tarantulas nor scorpions lay their eggs inside saguaros. Even if they did, a thousand of these baby critters would not have the strength to cause a saguaro to quiver and shake.

The Urban Legend: An Arizona Department of Public Safety (DPS) highway patrol vehicle came across a pile of smoldering metal imbedded in a cliff, on the outside curve of a road. At first, the officers thought it was the site of a plane crash. After careful analysis of the wreckage, DPS figured out what had happened. Someone had obtained a JATO (Jet Assisted Take-Off) unit. A JATO unit is a rocket-like device used by the military to allow large aircraft to takeoff from short runways. Attached to the side of the aircraft, it gives them an extra boost of thrust, enabling them to reach to takeoff speeds much faster. They attached the JATO rocket to a 1967 Chevy Impala, took the car out to a straight stretch of desolate highway, and fired off the rocket. Apparently the car went too fast and the driver was unable to stop before he encountered a curve in the road. The car's brakes were burned up, so he must have tried desperately to stop the car before the impact. DPS officials estimated that the car was going over 300 miles per hour when it crashed.

This urban legend, which sounds like a scene out of a "road-runner and coyote" cartoon, has been circulating for several years. Earlier versions placed the crash scene in New Mexico and California. In recent years, the crash takes place in Arizona. It's a good story, but it never happened. Several times a month someone calls the Arizona DPS to ask about the "rocket car." They have to tell the caller that it is just a myth.

The Urban Legend: When they were building Hoover Dam, several construction workers fell into the wet concrete poured to form the enormous walls of the dam. The concrete was like quicksand and these unfortunate souls quickly sank to their deaths. It was impossible to retrieve the bodies before the concrete hardened and they are embedded in the walls of the dam to this day.

Almost 100 people were killed and many more were injured during the construction of the Hoover Dam. However, there is no record of anyone drowning in the wet concrete or being entombed in this massive structure.

The Urban Legend: During the mid-1960s NASA trained astronauts in remote sections of northeastern Arizona. The terrain in parts of the area was similar to what Apollo astronauts expected to find on the moon. One of those training sessions was held near Tuba City, on the Navajo Reservation. A Navajo

sheepherder came upon this group of NASA technicians and potential astronauts. He watched curiously for a while, then approached one of the men from NASA.

"What are you doing?" the sheepherder asked.

"We're training astronauts to go to the moon." was the response.

The sheepherder watched a bit more then asked, "Could you send a message to the moon for me?"

The technicians discussed the proposal then agreed. They must have thought that this would make be an interesting story—a Native American sends a message to the moon. They brought over a tape recorder and told the sheepherder to speak in the microphone. Instead of using English, the man spoke briefly in Navajo. He thanked the men then wandered off toward his sheep. NASA was curious about what the message said so they took the tape recorder into Tuba City. They approached several Navajo residents, played back the tape, and asked them to translate. Each of them laughed at the message, but refused to translate it into English. Finally, they found someone who agreed to translate the message. Like the others he laughed, then said, "The message says: 'Watch out for these guys, they come to take your land.'"

This is a great story, which is supposed to be true, but there is no evidence that it ever happened.

The Urban Legend: Years ago, when there was a major slump in video game sales, the Atari Corporation dumped thousands of unsold game cartridges into a secret landfill in a desolate part of Arizona. Atari wanted to be sure that the cartridges could never be found and resold so they covered them with truckloads of wet concrete.

Although this legend still circulates the Internet, there is no evidence that it ever happened. If Atari wanted to dispose of surplus cartridges, there are cheaper ways of doing it than secretly hauling them to Arizona, digging a big hole, and covering them in concrete.

The Old West

Despite its name, a ten-gallon hat would hold less than one gallon of water. Although there a several theories about the origin of the term "ten-gallon hat," it probably originated from a fancy Mexican sombrero called a sombrero galon ("braided hat"). At some point, cowboys started to refer to large cowboy hats as "ten galonas." The word "ten" probably referring to a large hat size. Over the years the expression was further "Americanized" and large cowboy hats became known "ten-gallon hats."

You may be surprised to learn that the word "cowboy" did not originate in the old west. The first documented use of the word cowboy was during the Revolutionary War. It was used to describe loyalist soldiers and colonists who engaged in various raids and ambushes in the New York area. The most famous of these groups was "Delancy's Cowboys," commanded by Oliver Delancy.

ψ

In American culture, the name Wyatt Earp is almost synonymous with the word "lawman." In the movie "The Fugitive," when Tommy Lee Jones' character arrives on the seen and announces that he's taking over the investigation, the local Sheriff turns to his deputies and says: "OK boys were shutting it down. Wyatt Earp is here to mop things up." When the commander of the U. S. Marines landed in Somalia he proclaimed to his troops and the media: "This may be Dodge City, but we're Wyatt Earp!" This famous lawman has become legendary and has been portrayed in at least 30 movies. Earp has also been seen countless times on television. Whether it's an episode of Young Indiana Jones or Star Trek, Wyatt Earp is there whenever TV screenwriters need a heroic western lawman to be part of the story.

Was Earp really the incorruptible, upstanding lawman that he is often portrayed to be? Let's take a look at some reported facts. Despite his portrayal in books, films, and television, Earp never was the Marshal of Dodge City, Kansas or of Tombstone, Arizona. The highest office he ever held was that of Assistant Marshal. While he was a policeman in Kansas, he turned a blind eye to a prostitution ring that his brother James was rumored to be running. In 1871 Earp was indicted for stealing horses. He was involved in numerous street fights and shot (some would say murdered) several people out of vengeance. He was arrested in San Francisco for running an illegal gambling operation. He was charged (but never tried) on murder charges for his role in the "Shoot-out at the O.K. Corral." In Idaho, he was accused of "claim jumping." He was arrested in Alaska for interfering with local law enforcement officers trying to make an arrest. Three months later he was charged with assaulting a military policeman. Earp was also arraigned in Los Angeles for operating a "bunco game." It's true that, when he was acting as a lawman, he was considered to be both courageous and effective. However, his real life was very different from the legend.

The branding of cattle did not originate in the Old West. As early as the 1600s, cattle in New England were being branded.

In western movies real cowboys drank whiskey right out of the bottle. Kids, school marms, and "city slickers" drank sarsaparilla. You might have thought that sarsaparilla (often spelled, incorrectly, as sasparilla) was made from the sarsaparilla plant. It wasn't. The original formula for sarsaparilla was a combination of birch oil and sassafras.

ψ

In the mid 1800s, the United States formed the Camel Military Corp to determine if camels could be used as an alternative to horses in desert terrain of the southwest. Although a caravan of these beasts successfully crossed from Texas to California, the test was less than successful. The camels did not tolerate the rocky terrain very well and they tended to scare the horses and mules that accompanied the expedition. When the Camel Military Corp was disbanded some of the animals escaped into the desert. To this day, some people will tell you that descendants of the original camels roam remote areas of Arizona's deserts. However, if you expect to see a camel in the Arizona desert someday you're going to be disappointed. All of the escaped camels either died of natural causes or were shot by hunters and prospectors.

ψ

The "fastest gun in the west" was not always the one to survive a gunfight. Shooting straight was considered more important than shooting first. It was better to take a few fractions of a second longer to make sure that your aim was on-target. Some other false notions about gunfighters are: They shot from the hip. They fanned their guns. They fired both guns at once. While these techniques might have been fine for showing off, they weren't used by a successful gunfighter—one that wanted to survive a gunfight.

ψ

You may have seen cowboys in a western movie count how many times their opponent had fired during a gun battle. After they heard six shots, they knew he would have to re-load—a perfect time to jump out from behind that water barrel and gun the varmint down. In fact, many guns used in the old west weren't fully loaded. Due to the mechanism used in early revolvers, and because some guns had a "hair trigger," it was typical to load your six-shooter with only five bullets. The chamber under the hammer was not loaded to prevent accidental misfires.

ψ

Although we most often associate the tomahawk with Native Americans, it wasn't produced by these tribes. The word "tomahawk" is normally used to describe a metal war hatchet.

Early Native Americans did not have the technology to produce such weapons. Tomahawks were created by white craftsmen for trade with Native Americans.

Another misconception about the tomahawk is that it was a throwing weapon. Western movies and TV shows frequently show an Indian throwing his tomahawk at the "hero." Of course, the Indian always misses and the tomahawk sticks into a nearby tree or the side of a covered wagon. In reality, the tomahawk, when used as a weapon, was probably only wielded during close combat. Throwing one was too risky. If you missed you would have thrown away a valuable weapon.

When a bank robbery is shown in a western movie, masked robbers always burst into the bank with guns drawn. If the teller hesitates when he is told to open the safe, a couple of shots fired into the air will "motivate" him to move a little faster. In reality, most (successful) bank robbers were more discrete than this. The more attention that you drew to yourself, the more likely that the local sheriff would be waiting for you when you left to make your "getaway." Many robbers did not wear masks, and although they carried guns, these were usually left in their holsters or hidden beneath a jacket.

The Lone Ranger's "faithful Indian friend" Tonto always called the masked man "Kemosabe." For years a rumor has circulated that "Kemosabe" was a poor pronunciation of the Spanish phrase "quien no sabe." This phrase translates in English to "he who knows nothing." According to one version of the rumor, a Native American suggested the name to the show's producers, telling them that it was an Indian word that meant "friend." The word was really meant to be an insult, and he delighted in listening to the Indian character Tonto refer to this white man as "he who knows nothing." The truth is that the name Kemosabe was suggested by Jim Jewell, one of the directors of the Lone Ranger radio show. He got the name from a summer camp called "Kamp Kee-Mo Sah-Bee," which was run by his father-in-law.

When movie cowboys aren't in the local saloon they are always on horseback. Real cowboys rarely spent this much time on a horse. Most of their day was spent doing chores such as mending fences and stacking hay bales.

Bibliography

The following is a listing of some of the sources that were used to create this book.

Barnes, Will C. *Arizona Place Names.* Tucson: University of Arizona Press, 1988 (originally published in 1935).

Barr, Tom. *Unique Arizona.* Sante Fe, NM: John Muir Publications, 1994.

Bell, Bob Boze. *The Illustrated Life and Times of Doc Holliday.* Phoenix: Tri Star - Boze Publications, 1995.

Bell, Bob Boze. *The Illustrated Life and Times of Wyatt Earp.* Phoenix: Tri Star - Boze Publications, 1995.

Bell, Bob Boze *Outlaws & Gunfighters of the Wild West.* Phoenix: Tri Star - Boze Publications, 1999.

Carlson, Frances G. *Cave Creek and Carefree Arizona.* Scottsdale: Encanto Press, 1988.

Cheek, Lawrence W. *Arizona.* Oakland, CA: Compass American Guides, Inc., 1995.

Chronic, Halka. *Roadside Geology of Arizona.* Missoula MT: Mountain Press Publishing Company, 1981.

Chun, Claire, and others. *Ultimate Arizona.* Berkeley, CA: Ulysses Press, 1995.

Dillon, Richard. *Arizona's Amazing Towns: From Wild West to High Tech.* Tempe: Four Peaks Press, 1992.

Euler, Robert C, and Tikalsky, Frank. *The Grand Canyon: Intimate Views.* Tucson: The University of Arizona Press, 1992.

Fishbein, Seymour L. *Grand Canyon Country: Its Majesty and Its Lore.* Washington, D.C.: National Geographic Society, 1991.

Goff, John S. *Arizona: An Illustrated History of the Grand Canyon State.* Northridge, CA: Windsor Publications, Inc., 1988.

Hansen, Kevin. *Cougar, The American Lion.* Flagstaff: Northland Publishing, 1995.

Hoffmeister, Donald F. *Mammals of Arizona.* Tucson: The University of Arizona Press, 1986.

Jaeger, Edmund C. *Desert Wildlife.* Stanford, CA: Stanford University Press, 1961.

Klauber, Laurence M. *Rattlesnakes: Their Habits, Life Histories, & Influence on Mankind.* Berkeley, CA: University of California Press, 1982.

Larson, Peggy. *A Sierra Club Naturalists Guide: The Deserts of the Southwest.* San Francisco, CA: Sierra Club Books, 1977.

Lazaroff, David W. *Arizona-Sonora Desert Museum Book of Answers.* Tucson: Arizona-Sonora Desert Museum Press, 1998.

Lehman, Charles A. *Desert Survival Handbook.* Phoenix: Primer Publishers, 1993.

Lowe, Charles H., ed. *The Vertebrates of Arizona.* Tucson: The University of Arizona Press, 1972.

Luckingham, Bradford. Phoenix, *The History of a Southwestern Metropolis.* Tucson: The University of Arizona Press. 1989.

Phillips, Steven J. and Comus, Patricia W. ed. *A Natural History of the Sonoran Desert.* Tucson: Arizona-Sonora Desert Museum Press, 2000.

Sheridan, Thomas E. *Arizona: A History.* Tucson: The University of Arizona Press, 1995.

Sikorsky, Robert. *Fools Gold: The Facts, Myths and Legends of the Lost Dutchman Mine and the Superstition Mountains.* Phoenix: Golden West Publishers, 1983.

Smith, Robert L. *Venomous Animals of Arizona.* Tucson: The University of Arizona Press, 1992.

Smith, Zachary A., ed. *Politics and Public Policy in Arizona.* Westport, CT: Praeger Publishers, 1996

Stoops, Erik D. and Wright, Annette. *Snakes and Reptiles of the Southwest.* Phoenix: Golden West Publishers, 1993.

Trimble, Marshall. Arizona: *A Cavalcade of History.* Tucson: Treasure Chest Publications, 1990.

Trimble, Marshall. *Arizona Adventure.* Phoenix: Golden West Publishers, 1994.

Trimble, Marshall. *Marshall Trimble's Official Arizona Trivia.* Phoenix: Golden West Publishers, 1997.

Trimble, Marshall. *Roadside History of Arizona.* Missoula, MT: Mountain Press Publishing Company, 1986.

Tweit, Susan J. *The Great Southwest Nature Factbook.* Anchorage, AK: Alaska Northwest Books, 1992.

Werner, Floyd and Olson, Carl. *Insects of the Southwest.* Tucson: Fisher Books, 1994

Index